The Best of Mary Maxim®

Sweet Baby Blankets

LEISURE ARTS, INC. • Maumelle, Arkansas

Baby Flowers Blanket

◼◼◼◻ INTERMEDIATE

SHOPPING LIST

Yarn (DK/Sportweight)

[1.75 ounces, 160 yards
(50 grams, 146 meters) per ball]:

☐ White   5 balls
☐ Pink   3 balls
☐ Green   3 balls
☐ Aqua   3 balls

Crochet Hook

☐ Size G-6 (4.00 mm)

or size needed for gauge

SIZE INFORMATION

Finished: 38" x 41" [96.5 x 104 cm]

GAUGE INFORMATION

One hexagon measures 5.5" [14 cm] wide from point to point, and 3" [7.5 cm] wide from side to side, using **suggested** hook or any size hook which will give the correct gauge.

— STITCH GUIDE —

See page 30.

INSTRUCTIONS

Make Block in colors as given below.

Block 1: (make 9) Color 1- Aqua, Color 2- Pink, Color 3- Green.

Block 2: (make 9) Color 1-Green, Color 2-Aqua, Color 3-Pink.

Block 3: (make 11) Color 1-Pink, Color 2-Green, Color 3-Aqua.

Block 4: (make 9) Color 1- Aqua, Color 2- Green, Color 3-Pink.

Block 5: (make 9) Color 1-Pink, Color 2-Aqua, Color 3- Green.

Block 6: (make 12) Color 1-Green, Color 2- Pink, Color 3- Aqua.

Basic Block:

Using Color 1, ch 4, join with sl st in first ch to form a ring.

Rnd 1: Ch 3 (counts as first dc throughout), 2 dc in ring, [ch 2, 3 dc in ring] 5 times, ch 2, join with sl st in top of beg dc. (6 small petals made) Fasten off.

Rnd 2: Join Color 2 with sl st in any ch-2 sp, (ch 3, dc, ch 3, 2 dc) in same sp, [ch 1, (2 dc, ch 3, 2 dc) in next ch-2 sp] 5 times, ch 1, sl st in top of beg dc to join. (6 ch-3 sps)

Rnd 3: Sl st in each of next 2 dc and into ch-3 sp, ch 3, 9 dc in same sp, [10 dc in next ch-3 sp] 5 times, join with sl st in beg dc. (6 large petals made) Fasten off.

Rnd 4: Join Color 3 with sc in 2nd dc of any large petal, sc in each of next 8 dc, [dc in ch-1 sp of Rnd 2**, skip next dc, sc in each of next 9 dc] 5 times, but ending last rep at **, join with sl st in beg sc. Fasten off.

Rnd 5: Join White with sl st in any dc, ch 3, *dc in each of next 3 sc, tr in next sc, ch 1, tr in next sc, dc in each of next 5 sts; rep from * around, but ending last rep with dc in each of last 4 sc, join with sl st in beg dc.

Half Block:

Make 2 each following color sequence of Blocks 1, 2, 4 and 5.

Row 1: Using Color 1, ch 6 (first 5 ch count as [dc, ch 2]), ([3 dc, ch 2] 3 times, dc) in 6th ch from hook. Fasten off.

Row 2: With wrong side facing, join Color 2 with sl st in first ch-2 sp, ch 6 (counts as dc, ch 3), 2 dc in same sp, ch 1, [(2 dc, ch 3, 2 dc) in next ch-2 sp, ch 1] twice, (2 dc, ch 3, dc) in last ch-2 sp, turn.

Row 3: Sl st into ch-3 sp, ch 3, work 4 dc in same sp, 10 dc in each of the next 2 ch-3 sps, 5 dc in last ch-3 sp. Fasten off.

Row 4: With right side facing, join Color 3 with sc in first dc, sc in each of next 3 dc, skip next dc, [dc in ch-1 sp of Row 2, skip next dc, sc in each of next 9 dc] twice, dc in next ch-1 sp of Row 2, skip next dc, sc in each of last 4 dc. Fasten off.

Row 5: With right side facing, join White with sl st in first sc, ch 3, [dc in each of next 8 sts, tr in next sc, ch 1, tr in same sc] twice, dc in each of last 9 sts, ch 3, sc in last sc again, now working into ends of rows, work 3 hdc into each of next 2 rows, hdc in next row, work 2 dc into ring, hdc in next row, work 3 hdc into each of next 2 rows, dc into same st as join, sl st in top of beg ch-3. Fasten off.

To Assemble: Using Placement Diagram, with right sides of all motifs facing upwards, either using sc to join, or sewing together, join blocks in order indicated.

Border: With right side of blanket facing, join White with sl st in first free dc of the 2nd Motif at upper right corner.
Rnd 1: Ch 1, sc in same st, sc in next st, *[(2 dc, ch 3, 2 dc) in next st - **Shell made**, sc in each of next 4 sts] 4 times, but ending last rep with sc in each of last 2 sts of Motif, skip next join, sc in each of first 2 sts of next Motif; rep from * 4 times more across top edge of blanket, now work around Corner Motif as *Shell in next st, [sc in each of next 4 sts, Shell in next st] 5 times, sc in each of last 2 sts of Motif, skip next join,*

now working down side edge of blanket, **working across Half Block, work 2 sc in next ch-sp, skip next st, Shell in next st, [sc in each of next 4 sts, Shell in next st] 3 times, skip next st, 2 sc in next ch-sp, skip next join, sc in each of first 2 sts of next Motif***, Shell in next st, sc in each of next 4 sts, Shell in next st, sc in each of next 2 sts; rep from ** 3 times more, but

ending last rep at ***, now work around Corner Motif as before, now rep from * once more, but omit working the last 2 sts of the rep when you come around the last corner, join with sl st in first sc.
Rnd 2: Ch 1, sc in same st, 8 dc in next ch-3 sp, *skip next sc, sc in each of next 2 sc, 8 dc in next ch-3 sp; rep from * around to last 2 sc, skip next sc, sc in next sc, join with sl st in first sc. Fasten off.
Weave in all ends securely.

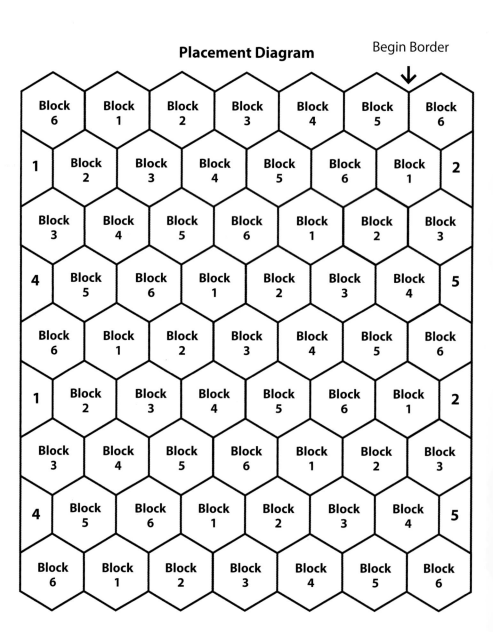

Placement Diagram   Begin Border
↓

Block 6	Block 1	Block 2	Block 3	Block 4	Block 5	Block 6
Block 2	Block 3	Block 4	Block 5	Block 6	Block 1
Block 3	Block 4	Block 5	Block 6	Block 1	Block 2	Block 3
Block 5	Block 6	Block 1	Block 2	Block 3	Block 4
Block 6	Block 1	Block 2	Block 3	Block 4	Block 5	Block 6
Block 2	Block 3	Block 4	Block 5	Block 6	Block 1
Block 3	Block 4	Block 5	Block 6	Block 1	Block 2	Block 3
Block 5	Block 6	Block 1	Block 2	Block 3	Block 4
Block 6	Block 1	Block 2	Block 3	Block 4	Block 5	Block 6

Cushy Crocheted Blanket

Shown on page 7.

■■■□ INTERMEDIATE

SHOPPING LIST

Yarn (Worsted Weight) MEDIUM 4

[6 ounces, 342 yards
(170 grams, 312 meters) per skein]:

☐ Buttercup   5 skeins

Crochet Hook

☐ Size H-8 (5.00 mm)
   or size needed for gauge

SIZE INFORMATION

Finished: 38" [96.5 cm] square

GAUGE INFORMATION

5 dc and 8 rows to 4" [10 cm]
measured over pattern, using
suggested hook or any size hook
which will give the correct gauge.

── STITCH GUIDE ──

Pdc   Yo, insert hook from front
to back to front, around post of
indicated st, yo and draw up a loop,
yo and pull through 2 loops] twice.

Back Loop Only

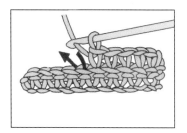

Post Stitches

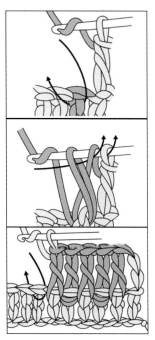

INSTRUCTIONS

Note: Begin at center of Blanket and
work outwards.

Ch 4, join with a sl st in first ch to form
a ring.

Rnd 1: Ch 3 (counts as first dc
throughout), 2 dc in ring,
[ch 1, 3 dc in ring] 3 times,
sc in top of 1st dc to form last ch-1 sp.
(12 dc and 4 ch-1 sps)

Rnd 2: Ch 2 (counts as first hdc
throughout), FPdc around each of
next 3 sts, *(hdc, ch 1, hdc) in
next ch-1 sp - **corner made**,
FPdc around each of next 3 dc;
rep from * twice more,
hdc in same st as first hdc,
sc in first hdc to form last ch-1 sp.

Rnd 3: Ch 2, FPdc around each of next
5 sts, *make corner, FPdc around each
of next 5 sts; rep from * twice more,
hdc in next ch-1 sp, sc in first hdc to
form last ch-1 sp.

Rnd 4: Work as Rnd 3, but work FPdc
around each of next 7 sts. (36 sts and
4 ch-1 sps)

Rnd 5: Ch 2, hdc in *back loop only* of
each of next 9 sts, *make corner, hdc
in *back loop only* of each of next 9 sts;
rep from * twice more, hdc in next
ch-1 sp, sc in first hdc to form
last ch-1 sp.

Rnd 6: Ch 2, *FPdc around next hdc,
sc in *back loop only* of each of
next 9 hdc, FPdc around next hdc,
make corner; rep from * 3 times
more, ending last rep with hdc in
last ch-1 sp, sc in first hdc to form last
ch-1 sp.

Rnd 7: Ch 2, *FPdc around each of
next 2 sts, sc in *back loop only* of each
of next 9 sc, FPdc around each of next
2 sts, make corner; rep from * 3 times
more, ending last rep with hdc in last
ch-1 sp, sc in first hdc to form
last ch-1 sp.

Rnd 8: Ch 2, *FPdc around each of
next 3 sts, sc in *back loop only* of each
of next 9 sc, FPdc around each of next
3 sts, make corner; rep from * 3 times
more, ending last rep with hdc in
last ch-1 sp, sc in 1st hdc to form
last ch-1 sp.

Rnd 9: Ch 2, *FPdc around each of next 4 sts, sc in *back loop only* of each of next 9 sc, FPdc around each of next 4 sts, make corner; rep from * 3 times, ending last rep with hdc in last ch-1 sp, sc in first hdc to form last ch-1 sp.

Rnd 10: Ch 2, *FPdc around each of next 5 sts, sc in *back loop only* of each of next 9 sc, FPdc around each of next 5 sts, make corner; rep from * 3 times, ending last rep with hdc in last ch-1 sp, sc in first hdc to form last ch-1 sp.

Rnd 11: Ch 2, *FPdc around each of next 6 sts, sc in *back loop only* of each of next 9 sc, FPdc around each of next 6 sts, make corner; rep from * 3 times, ending last rep with hdc in last ch-1 sp, sc in first hdc to form last ch-1 sp.

Rnd 12: Ch 2, *FPdc around each of next 7 sts, sc in *back loop only* of each of next 9 sc, FPdc around each of next 7 sts, make corner; rep from * 3 times, ending last rep with hdc in last ch-1 sp, sc in first hdc to form last ch-1 sp.

Rnd 13: Ch 2, *FPdc around each of next 8 sts, sc in *back loop only* of each of next 9 sc, FPdc around each of next 8 sts, make corner; rep from * 3 times, ending last rep with hdc in last ch-1 sp, sc in first hdc to form last ch-1 sp.

Rnd 14: Ch 2, *sc in *back loop only* of each of next 9 sts, hdc in both loops of each of next 9 sc, sc in *back loop only* of each of next 9 sts, make corner; rep from * 3 times, ending last rep with hdc in last ch-1 sp, sc in first hdc to form last ch-1 sp.

Rnd 15: Ch 2, *FPdc around next st, sc in *back loop only* of each of next 9 sts, FPdc around each of next 9 sts, sc in *back loop only* of each of next 9 sts, FPdc around next st, make corner; rep from * 3 times, ending last rep with hdc in last ch-1 sp, sc in first hdc to form last ch-1 sp.

Rnd 16: Ch 2, *FPdc around each of next 2 sts, sc in *back loop only* of each of next 9 sc, FPdc around each of next 9 sts, sc in *back loop only* of each of next 9 sc, FPdc around each of next 2 sts, make corner; rep from * 3 times, ending last rep with hdc in last ch-1 sp, sc in first hdc to form last ch-1 sp.

Rnd 17: Ch 2, *FPdc around each of next 3 sts, sc in *back loop only* of each of next 9 sc, FPdc around each of next 9 sts, sc in *back loop only* of each of next 9 sc, FPdc around each of next 3 sts, make corner; rep from * 3 times, ending last rep with hdc in last ch-1 sp, sc in first hdc to form last ch-1 sp.

Rnd 18: Ch 2, *FPdc around each of next 4 sts, sc in *back loop only* of each of next 9 sc, FPdc around each of next 9 sts, sc in *back loop only* of each of next 9 sc, FPdc around each of next 4 sts, make corner; rep from * 3 times, ending last rep with hdc in last ch-1 sp, sc in first hdc to form last ch-1 sp.

Rnd 19: Ch 2, *FPdc around each of next 5 sts, sc in *back loop only* of each of next 9 sc, FPdc around each of next 9 sts, sc in *back loop only* of each of next 9 sc, FPdc around each of next 5 sts, make corner; rep from * 3 times, ending last rep with hdc in last ch-1 sp, sc in first hdc to form last ch-1 sp.

Rnd 20: Ch 2, *FPdc around each of next 6 sts, sc in *back loop only* of each of next 9 sc, FPdc around each of next 9 sts, sc in *back loop only* of each of next 9 sc, FPdc around each of next 6 sts, make corner; rep from * 3 times, ending last rep with hdc in last ch-1 sp, sc in first hdc to form last ch-1 sp.

Rnd 21: Ch 2, *FPdc around each of next 7 sts, sc in *back loop only* of each of next 9 sc, FPdc around each of next 9 sts, sc in *back loop only* of each of next 9 sc, FPdc around each of next 7 sts, make corner; rep from * 3 times, ending last rep with hdc in last ch-1 sp, sc in first hdc to form last ch-1 sp.

Rnd 22: Ch 2, *FPdc around each of next 8 sts, sc in *back loop only* of each of next 9 sc, FPdc around each of next 9 sts, sc in *back loop only* of each of next 9 sc, FPdc around each of next 8 sts, make corner; rep from * 3 times, ending last rep with hdc in last ch-1 sp, sc in first hdc to form last ch-1 sp.

Rnd 23: Ch 2, *sc in *back loop only* of each of next 9 sts, [hdc in both loops of each of next 9 sts, sc in *back loop only* of each of next 9 sts] twice, make corner; rep from * 3 times, ending last rep with hdc in last ch-1 sp, sc in first hdc to form last ch-1 sp.

Rnd 24: Ch 2, *FPdc around next st, sc in *back loop only* of each of next 9 sc, [FPdc around each of next 9 sts, sc in *back loop only* of each of next 9 sts] twice, FPdc around next st, make corner; rep from * 3 times, ending last rep with hdc in last ch-1 sp, sc in first hdc to form last ch-1 sp.

Rnd 25: Ch 2, *FPdc around each of next 2 sts, sc in *back loop only* of each of next 9 sc, [FPdc around each of next 9 sts, sc in *back loop only* of each of next 9 sts] twice, FPdc around each of next 2 sts, make corner; rep from * 3 times, ending last rep with hdc in last ch-1 sp, sc in first hdc to form last ch-1 sp. Now continue in pattern as set, alternating sc in back loops only and FPdc, working until there are 8 FPdc to begin and end each side, and having an additional repeat (instructions in square brackets), for each section of blocks. Work until you have 7 "blocks" of sc in back loop only and 6 "blocks" of FPdc on each side. When you have completed this section, including the rnd with 8 FPdc to begin and end each side, Do Not finish off.

Border:

Rnd 1: Ch 1, 2 sc in same sp, *ch 1, skip next st, sc in next st; rep from * to corner, adjusting sts if necessary to end with ch 1, 3 sc in corner ch-1 sp; rep from * around, ending with sc in beg corner ch-1 sp, join with sl st in 1st sc.

Rnd 2: Ch 2, hdc in same st, now hdc in each sc and ch-1 sp around, working 3 hdc in center sc in the corner 3-sc, join with sl st in first hdc.
Break yarn and fasten off.
Weave in all ends.

Bavarian Baby Blanket

Shown on page 11.

SHOPPING LIST

Yarn (DK /Sport Weight) 〔LIGHT 3〕
[1.75 ounces, 160 yards
(50 grams, 146 meters) per ball]:

☐ Color 1   Blue   2 balls
☐ Color 2   Aqua   2 balls
☐ Color 3   Purple   2 balls
☐ Color 4   Melon   3 balls
☐ Color 5   Yellow   2 balls
☐ Color 6   Green   2 balls

Crochet Hook
☐ Size G-6 (4.0 mm)
    or size needed for gauge

SIZE INFORMATION
Finished: 29" x 44" [73.5 x 111.5 cm]

GAUGE INFORMATION
Three 9-tr groups (or 3 repeats of pattern) to 5.5" [14 cm] and 6 bands of color to 6.75" [17 cm], measured over pattern using **suggested** hook or any size hook needed to obtain correct gauge.

─── STITCH GUIDE ───

4-FPtr CL   *Yo twice, insert hook around post of next tr, from front to back to front and draw up a loop, yo and draw through 2 loops on hook] twice; rep from * 3 times more, yo and draw through all 5 loops on hook.

FPhdc   Yo hook, insert hook around post of stitch indicated, from front to back to front, and draw up a loop, yo and draw through all loops on hook.

5-FPtr CL   *Yo twice, insert hook around post of next tr, from front to back to front and draw up a loop, [yo and draw through 2 loops on hook] twice; rep from * 4 times more, yo and draw through all 6 loops on hook.

9-FPtr CL   *Yo twice, insert hook around post of next tr, from front to back to front and draw up a loop, [yo and draw through 2 loops on hook] twice; rep from * 3 times more**, yo twice, insert hook around post of next hdc as before and draw up a loop, [yo and draw through 2 loops on hook] twice, now rep from * to ** once more, yo and draw through all 10 loops on hook.

─────────────

INSTRUCTIONS
Using Color 1, ch 153.
Row 1 (right side) :
Hdc in 3rd ch from hook,
*skip next 4 ch, 9 tr in next ch,
skip next 4 ch, hdc in next ch;
rep from * across, turn. (15 9-tr groups)

Row 2: Change to Color 2 , ch 3, 4-FPtr CL over next 4 tr, ch 4, FPhdc around next tr, *ch 4, work 9-FPtr CL *over next (4 tr, hdc, and 4 tr),* ch 4, FPhdc over next tr; rep from * 13 more times, ch 4, 5-FPtr CL over last 5 sts, turn.

Row 3: Ch 4, 4 tr in top of first CL, hdc in next hdc, *9 tr in center of next CL, hdc in next hdc; rep from * 13 more times, 5 tr in top of last CL, turn.

Row 4: Change to Color 3, ch 1, FPhdc over first tr, *ch 4, work 9-FPtr CL, ch 4, FPhdc over next tr, rep from * across, ending last rep with FPhdc around last tr, turn.

Row 5: Ch 2 (counts as first hdc), *9 tr in center of first CL, hdc in next hdc; rep from * across, turn.

Rows 6 and 7: Change to Color 4 and rep Rows 2 and 3.

Rows 8 and 9: Change to Color 5 and rep Rows 4 and 5.

Rows 10 and 11: Change to Color 6 and rep Rows 2 and 3.

Rows 12 and 13: Change to Color 1 and rep Rows 4 and 5.

Now rep Rows 2-13 five times more, but end last rep after Row 12.
Fasten off.
Weave in all ends securely.

Border: With right side of blanket facing, join Color 4 with sl st in upper right corner, in base of last FPhdc.

Rnd 1: Ch 1, sc in same st, *[ch 3, sc in next ch-4 sp, ch 3, sc in top of next CL, ch 3, sc in next ch-sp] 15 times, ch 3, sc in base of last FPhdc at end of row, now working along side edge, [ch 3, sc in base of next row] 53 times; rep from * once more, but omit last sc and join with sl st in first sc.

Rnd 2: Sl st in first ch-3 sp, ch 3 (counts as first dc), 6 dc in same sp, sc in next ch-3 sp, *7 dc in next ch-3 sp - **Shell made**, sc in next ch-3 sp; rep from * around, join with sl st in top of beg dc, turn.

Rnd 3: Sc in first dc of next Shell, *[ch 3, sl st in next dc] 6 times, skip next sc, sl st in first dc of next Shell; rep from * around, ending last rep with sl st in first sc.

Fasten off.

Weave in all ends.

Enlarged View of Border

Baby Pineapples Blanket

SHOPPING LIST

Yarn (Dk/ Sport Weight) 🌀FINE 2

[1.75 ounces, 171 yards
(50 grams, 158 meters) per ball]:

☐ White   6 balls

Crochet Hook

☐ Size G-6 (4.00 mm)
or size needed for gauge

SIZE INFORMATION

Finished: 32" x 44" [81.5 x 112 cm]

GAUGE INFORMATION

2 Shells + 2 ch-sps to 5" [12.5 cm] and
8 rows to 3.5" [9 cm] using **suggested**
hook or any size hook which will give
the correct stitch gauge.

——— STITCH GUIDE ———

V-st   (Dc, ch 2, dc) in stitch or space
indicated.

Shell   (2 dc, ch 2, 2 dc) in stitch or
space indicated.

{ }   Repeat the instructions given
between brackets the number of
times stated directly after last bracket.

INSTRUCTIONS

Ch 97.

Row 1: Sc in 7th ch from hook
(skipped ch count as turning ch),
*ch 3, skip next 3 ch, sc in next ch;
rep from * across to last 2 ch, ch 2,
skip next ch, dc in last ch, turn.

Row 2: Ch 1, sc in first dc, *7 dc in
next ch-3 sp**, sc in next ch-3 sp,
ch 3, sc in next ch-3 sp; rep from
* across, ending last rep at **,
skip next 2 ch of turning ch, sc in
next ch, turn.

Row 3: Ch 5 (counts as dc, ch 2),
skip first sc and next dc, *sc in next dc,
ch 3, skip next 3 dc, sc in next dc**,
ch 3, sc in next ch-3 sp, ch 3, skip
next dc; rep from * across, ending
last rep at **, ch 2, dc in last sc, turn.
Repeat Rows 2 and 3 until a total
of 65 rows have been completed.
Do not break yarn.

Border:

Rnd 1: Ch 4 (counts as hdc, ch 2),
hdc in same st as turning ch,
*hdc in next sc, (3 hdc in next ch-sp,
hdc in next sc) across to next corner,
work (*hdc, ch 2, hdc*) in last hdc -
corner made, now working in ends of
rows, hdc in same st as corner,
(2 hdc in next ch-sp, hdc in
next sc) across to next corner,
corner in corner st; rep from *
once more, omitting last corner,
join with sl st in 2nd ch of beg ch-4 -
89 hdc on each end and 99 hdc on
each side (not including corners).

Rnd 2: Sl st in corner sp, (*ch 3, dc, ch 2,
2 dc*) in corner sp - **beg corner made**,
*ch 1, skip next 2 sts, [V-st in next st,
ch 1, skip next 3 sts] 9 times,
[V-st in next st, ch 1, skip next 4 sts]
twice,
[V-st in next st, ch 1, skip next 3 sts]
10 times,
Shell in corner ch-2 sp - **corner made**,
ch 1, skip next hdc, V-st in next hdc,
[ch 1, skip next 2 hdc, V-st in next hdc]
32 times,
ch 1, corner in next corner sp; rep
from * once more, omitting corner on
last rep, join with sl st in top of
beg ch - 33 V-sts on each side and
21 V-sts on each end.

Rnd 3: Sl st to corner sp, work beg corner in same sp, *ch 3, skip first V-st, {9 tr in next V-st, ch 3, skip next 2 V-sts, Shell in next V-st, ch 3, skip next 2 V-sts} 3 times, 9 tr in next V-st, ch 3, skip next V-st, corner in corner, ch 3, skip next V-st, rep from { to } 5 times, 9 tr in next V-st, ch 3, skip next V-st, corner in corner; rep from * once more, omitting last corner, join as before.

Rnd 4: Sl st to corner sp, work beg corner in same sp, *{ch 2, dc in first tr, (ch 1, dc in next tr) 8 times, ch 2, Shell in ch-2 sp of next Shell} 3 times, ch 2, dc in first tr, (ch 1, dc in next tr) 8 times, ch 2, corner in corner, rep from { to } 5 times, ch 2, dc in first tr, (ch 1, dc in next tr) 8 times, ch 2, corner in corner; rep from * once more, omitting last corner, join as before.

Rnd 5: Sl st to corner sp, *(ch 3, dc, [ch 2, 2 dc] twice) in same sp - **beg corner made**, ch 2, *{sc in first ch-1 sp, [ch-3, sc in next ch-1 sp] 7 times, ch 2, Shell in ch-2 sp of next Shell, ch 2}, 3 times, sc in first ch-1 sp, [ch-3, sc in next ch-1 sp] 7 times, ch 2, *(2 dc, [ch 2, 2 dc] twice) in corner sp - **corner made**, ch 2, rep from { to } 5 times, sc in first ch-1 sp, [ch-3, sc in next ch-1 sp] 7 times, ch 2, corner in next corner; rep from * once more, omitting last corner, join as before.

Rnd 6: Sl st to first sp, (ch 3, dc, ch 2, 2 dc) in same sp, ch 3, Shell in next ch-2 sp, ch 2, *{sc in first ch-3 sp, [ch 3, sc in next ch-3 sp] 6 times, ch 2, (2 dc, [ch 2, 2 dc] twice) in ch-2 sp of next Shell, ch 2} 3 times, sc in first ch-3 sp, [ch 3, sc in next ch-3 sp] 6 times, ch 2, *Shell in first ch-2 sp of corner, ch 3, Shell in next ch-2 sp of corner, ch 2 - **corner made**, rep from { to } 5 times, sc in first ch-3 sp, [ch 3, sc in next ch-3 sp] 6 times, ch 2, corner in next corner; rep from * once more, omitting last corner, join as before.

Rnd 7: Sl st to first sp, (ch 3, dc, ch 2, 2 dc) in same sp, ch 3, sc in next ch-3 sp, ch 3, Shell in next ch-2 sp, ch 2, *{sc in first ch-3 sp, [ch 3, sc in next ch-3 sp] 5 times, ch 2, skip next ch-2 sp, Shell in next ch-2 sp, ch 3, Shell in next ch-2 sp, ch 2} 3 times, sc in first ch-3 sp, [ch 3, sc in next ch-3 sp] 5 times, ch 2, *Shell in ch-2 sp of next Shell, ch 3, sc in next ch-3 sp, ch 3, Shell in ch-2 sp of next Shell - **corner made**, ch 2, rep from { to } 5 times, sc in first ch-3 sp, [ch 3, sc in next ch-3 sp] 5 times, ch 2, corner in next corner; rep from * once more, omitting last corner, join as before.

Rnd 8: Sl st to first sp, (ch 3, dc, ch 2, 2 dc) in same sp, [ch 3, sc in next ch-3 sp] twice, ch 3, Shell in next ch-2 sp of next Shell, ch 2, *{sc in first ch-3 sp, [ch 3, sc in next ch-3 sp] 4 times, ch 2, Shell in ch-2 sp of next Shell, ch 3, sc in next ch-3 sp, ch 3, Shell in ch-2 sp of next Shell, ch 2} 3 times, sc in first ch-3 sp, [ch 3, sc in next ch-3 sp] 4 times, ch 2, *Shell in ch-2 sp of next Shell, [ch 3, sc in next ch-3 sp] twice, ch 3, Shell in ch-2 sp of next Shell - **corner made**, ch 2, rep from { to } 5 times, sc in first ch-3 sp, [ch 3, sc in next ch-3 sp] 4 times, ch 2; rep from * once more, omitting last corner, join as before.

Rnd 9: Sl st to first sp, (ch 3, dc, ch 2, 2 dc) in same sp, ch 3, sc in first ch-3 sp, 7 dc in next ch-3 sp, sc in next ch-3 sp, ch 3, Shell in ch-2 sp of next Shell, ch 2, *{sc in first ch-3 sp, [ch 3, sc in next ch-3 sp] 3 times, ch 2, Shell in ch-2 sp of next Shell, [ch 3, sc in next ch-3 sp] twice, ch 3, Shell in ch-2 sp of next Shell, ch 2} 3 times, sc in first ch-3 sp, [ch 3, sc in next ch-3 sp] 3 times, ch 2, *Shell in ch-2 sp of next Shell, ch 3, sc in first ch-3 sp, ch 1, 7 dc in next ch-3 sp, ch 1, sc in next ch-3 sp, ch 3, Shell in ch-2 sp of next Shell - **corner made**, ch 2, rep from { to } 5 times, sc in first ch-3 sp, [ch 3, sc in next ch-3 sp] 3 times, ch 2, corner in next corner; rep from * once more, omitting last corner, join as before.*

Rnd 10: Sl st to first sp, (ch 3, dc, ch 2, 2 dc) in same sp, ch 3, sc in next ch-3 sp, ch 2, dc in first dc, [ch 1, dc in next dc] 6 times, ch 2, sc in next ch-3 sp, ch 3, Shell in ch-2 sp of next Shell, ch 1, *{sc in first ch-3 sp, [ch 3, sc in next ch-3 sp] twice, ch 1, Shell in ch-2 of next Shell, ch 3, sc in first ch-3 sp, ch 1, 7 dc in next ch-3 sp, ch 1, sc in next ch-3 sp, ch 3, Shell in ch-2 sp of next Shell, ch 1} 3 times, sc in first ch-3 sp, [ch 3, sc in next ch-3 sp] twice, ch 1, *Shell in ch-2 sp of next Shell, ch 3, sc in next ch-3 sp, ch 3, dc in first dc, [ch 1, dc in next dc] 6 times, ch 3, sc in next ch-3 sp, ch 3, Shell in ch-2 sp of next Shell - **corner made**, ch 1, rep from { to } 5 times, sc in first ch-3 sp, [ch 3, sc in next ch-3 sp] twice, ch 1, corner in next corner; rep from * once more, omitting last corner, join as before.*

Rnd 11: Sl st to first ch-sp, ch 4, dc in same sp, [ch 3, sc in next ch-3 sp] twice, ch 3, sc in first ch-1 sp, [ch 3, sc in next ch-1 sp] 5 times, [ch 3, sc in next ch-3 sp] twice, ch 3, V-st in ch-2 sp of next Shell, ch 1, *{sc in next ch-3 sp, ch 3, sc in next ch-3 sp, ch 1, V-st in ch-2 sp of next Shell, ch 3, sc in next ch-3 sp, ch 3, sc in next ch-1 sp, [ch 3, skip next dc, dc in next dc] 3 times, ch 3, sc in next ch-1 sp, ch 3, sc in next ch-3 sp, ch 3, V-st in ch-2 sp of next Shell, ch 1} 3 times, sc in next ch-3 sp, ch 3, sc in next ch-3 sp, ch 1, *V-st in ch-2 sp of next Shell, [ch 3, sc in next ch-3 sp] twice, ch 3, sc in first ch-1 sp, [ch 3, sc in next ch-1 sp] 5 times, [ch 3, sc in next ch-3 sp] twice, ch 3, V-st in ch-2 sp of next Shell -* **corner made**, ch 1, rep from { to } 5 times, sc in next ch-3 sp, ch 3, sc in next ch-3 sp, ch 1, corner in next corner; rep from * once more, omitting last corner, join as before.

Rnd 12: Sl st in first ch-sp, *ch 3, sc in next ch-sp; rep from * around, join with sl st in base of beg ch-3. Break yarn and fasten off. Weave in all ends.

Dreamy Baby Blanket

■■■☐ INTERMEDIATE

SHOPPING LIST

Yarn (Dk/ Sport Weight)

[1.75 ounces, 171 yards
(50 grams, 158 meters) per ball]:

☐ White (MC)   4 balls
☐ Blue or Pink (CC 1)   4 balls
☐ Mint (CC 2)   4 balls

Crochet Hook

☐ Size I-9 (5.50 mm)
   or size needed for gauge

SIZE INFORMATION

Finished: 38" [96.5 cm] diameter

GAUGE INFORMATION

Rnds 1-4 = 7.75" [19.5 cm] in
diameter using 2 strands of yarn and
suggested hook or any size hook
which will give the correct gauge.

—— STITCH GUIDE ——

3-dc CL   [Yo, insert hook and draw
up a loop, yo and draw through
2 loops on hook] 3 times, yo and
draw through all 4 loops on hook.

Note: Entire Blanket is worked using
2 strands of yarn.

INSTRUCTIONS

Using 2 strands of CC 2 held together,
ch 5, join with a sl st in first ch to form
a ring.

Rnd 1: Ch 2, [yo, insert hook in ring
and draw up a loop, yo and draw
through 2 loops on hook] twice,
yo and draw through all 3 loops on
hook, ch 3,
[3-dc CL in ring, ch 3] 7 times,
join with sl st in top of Beg 3-dc CL.
Fasten off. (8 CL's and 8 ch-3 sps)

Rnd 2: Join 2 strands of MC with sl st
in any ch-3 sp,
(ch 3 2 dc, ch 3, 3 dc) in same sp, ch 7,
sl st in last dc made,
*(3 dc, ch 3, 3 dc) in next ch-3 sp, ch 7,
sl st in last dc made;
rep from * 6 times, join with sl st
in first dc.

Note: Leave ch-7 loops unattached
as you work each rnd. They will be
worked together later.

Rnd 3: Sl st in next dc (2nd dc of
3-dc group), ch 3, dc in next dc,
(2 dc, ch 3, 2 dc) in ch-3 sp -
Shell made,
dc in each of next 2 dc, ch 7,
sl st in last dc made,
[skip next 2 dc (includes dc with ch-7
attached), dc in each of next 2 dc,
Shell in ch-3 sp, dc in each of
next 2 dc, ch 7, sl st in last dc made]
 7 times, join with sl st in first dc.
(8 Shells, 8 ch-7 sps)

Rnd 4: Sl st in next dc (2nd dc of
group), ch 3, dc in each dc to next
ch-3 sp, Shell in ch-3 sp,
dc in each dc to last dc of this group,
skip last dc,
ch 7, sl st in last dc made,
[skip next dc,
dc in each dc to next ch-3 sp,
Shell in ch-3 sp,
dc in each dc to last dc of this group,
skip last dc, ch 7, sl st in last dc made]
7 times, join with sl st in first dc.
Fasten off.

Rnds 5-7: Using 2 strands of CC 1
held together, rep Rnd 4.
(6 dc on either side of each Shell at
end of Rnd 7)
Fasten off.

Continue to rep Rnd 4 for pattern
(having one more st each side of Shell
on each rnd), and alternating colors
every 3 rnds as follows:
Work 3 rnds CC 2.
Work 3 rnds MC.
Work 3 rnds CC 1.
Work 3 rnds CC 2.
Work 3 rnds MC.
Work only 2 rnds CC 1.
Before working next rnd, remove
hook from working loop and draw
out to make a large loop for the
moment.

Now starting at any ch-7 loop of Rnd 2, working from center of blanket out, begin to lock the loops tog as follows: *insert hook in ch-7 loop, then catch ch-7 loop of next rnd and pull it through loop on hook, taking care that loops are not twisted; rep from * out to last rnd, remove hook and leave loop for last rnd.

Repeat for each section of ch-7 loops. Now insert hook back through working loop of last rnd worked.

Last Rnd: Sl st in next dc (2nd dc of group), ch 3, dc in each dc to next ch-3 sp, Shell in ch-3 sp, dc in each dc to last dc of this group, skip last dc, sl st in next ch-7 loop, [skip next dc, dc in each dc to next ch-3 sp, Shell in ch-3 sp, dc in each dc to last dc of this group, skip last dc, sl st in next ch-7 loop] 7 times, join with sl st in first dc.

Fasten off.

Weave in all ends.

Candy Stripes Blanket

Shown on page 21.

Shown on page 21.

 **EASY**

SHOPPING LIST

Yarn (Worsted Weight) MEDIUM 4

[3.5 ounces, 251 yards
(100 grams, 229 meters) per ball]:

☐ Any Color   5 balls

Crochet Hook

☐ Size 7 (4.50 mm)
  or size needed for gauge

SIZE INFORMATION

Finished: 32" x 40" [81.5 x 101.5 cm]

GAUGE INFORMATION

4 Blocks (each Block is ch 3, 3 dc) = 3.5"
[9 cm] across, using **suggested** hook
or any size hook which will give the
correct gauge or tension.

— STITCH GUIDE —

Note: Blanket is worked in rows
diagonally from corner to corner
(See Row Diagram, page 20).

INSTRUCTIONS

Row 1: Ch 6,
dc in 4th ch from hook (3 skipped ch
count as turning ch-sp), and each of
next 2 ch - **Beg Block made**.
Row 1 is complete.

Row 2: Ch 6, turn (flip previous block
so the turning ch-sp is at top of work),
dc in 4th ch from hook and each of
next 2 ch - Beg Block of 2nd Row
made *(Fig. 1a)*. Hold previous Block
close to last block made, and sl st in
turning ch-sp (which is at top of block),
ch 3, 3 dc in same sp - **Block made
(Fig. 1b)**. Row 2 is complete.

Fig. 1a

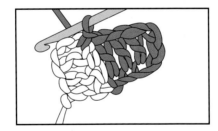

Fig. 1b

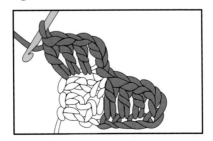

Row 3: Ch 6, turn as before, work
a Beg Block as in Row 1, then
work 2 Blocks. Row 3 is complete.

Row 4: Ch 6, turn as before, work
a Beg Block, work 3 Blocks.
Row 4 is complete.

Row 5: Join Color B with a sl st in
last dc made, ch 6, turn as before,
work a Beg Block, work 4 Blocks.
Row 5 is complete.

Continue in this manner, having one
more Block per row, until 41 rows
have been completed.

Row 42: Do Not work a Beg Block,
turn as before and sl st in each of last
3 dc of last block made in Row 41,
ch 3, 3 dc in same space, complete
row as before.

Row 43: Ch 6, turn, work a Beg Block,
complete row as before.

Rows 44, 46, 48, 50 and 52: Turn,
sl st in each of next 3 dc and into
ch-3 space, ch 3, work 3 dc in same
space, complete row as before.

Rows 45, 47, 49 and 51: Work as
Row 4, inc along right side of blanket.

Row 53: Do Not make a Beg Block,
turn, sl st in each of last 3 dc of last
Block made in Row 52, sl st into
ch-3 space of next Block, ch 3, 3 dc in
same space, complete row as before.
Now continue, starting each row with
slip st to ch-3 space - there are no
more Beg Blocks, and each row will
have one less block than the
previous row.

At the end of the last row,
there will be only one Block.
Break yarn and fasten off.

19

Border:

With right side facing, attach yarn with a sl st in upper right corner of afghan.

Rnd 1: Ch 3, 6 dc in same st, sc in next sp between blocks, *7 dc in next sp between blocks, sc in next sp between blocks; rep from * around entire outside edge of blanket, ending with a sl st in first dc. Fasten off.

Row Diagram

Row 4			
Row 3	Row 4		
Row 2	Row 3	Row 4	
Row 1	Row 2	Row 3	Row 4

(turning ch-sp marked at the end of each row's block)

Little Boy Blue Blanket

◼◼◼◻ INTERMEDIATE

SIZE INFORMATION

Finished: 40" [101.5 cm] square

GAUGE INFORMATION

One pattern repeat (V-st, Shell)
to 2" [5 cm] and 6 rows to 4" [10
cm] measured over pattern using
suggested hook or any size hook
which will give the correct gauge.

─── STITCH GUIDE ───

V-st   [Dc, ch 1, dc] all in indicated st
or space.
Shell   Work 5 dc in indicated st or
space.

INSTRUCTIONS

Using CC 1, ch 121.
Row 1: Dc in 5th ch from hook
(skipped ch count as ch 1, dc, ch 1),
*ch 1, skip next ch, dc in next ch;
rep from * to end, turn.
(59 ch-1 sps and 60 dc)
Row 2: Ch 4 (counts as dc, ch 1
throughout), dc in next dc,
*skip next ch-1 sp,
V-st in next ch-1 sp, skip next ch-1 sp,
Shell in next ch-1 sp;
rep from * to last 2 ch-1 sps,
skip next ch-1 sp, dc in next dc,
ch 1, skip next ch-1 sp,
dc in 3rd ch of beg ch-5, turn.
(14 V-sts and 14 Shells)
Row 3: Ch 4, dc in next dc,
[V-st in 3rd dc of next Shell,
Shell in ch-1 sp of next V-st] 14 times,
dc in next dc, ch 1, dc in last dc, turn.
Row 4: As Row 3.
Fasten off.
Row 5: Join MC with sl st in last dc
worked and rep Row 3.
Rows 6 and 7: Repeat Row 3.
Row 8: Join CC 2 with sl st in last dc
worked and rep Row 3.
Rows 9 and 10: Repeat Row 3.
Row 11: Join CC 1 with sl st in last dc
worked and rep Row 3.

Rows 12 and 13: Repeat Row 3.
Now continue to rep Row 3 for
pattern and work 3 rows of pattern in
each color as set until 18 stripes have
been completed, ending with CC 2.
Do Not fasten off.
Next Row: Ch 4, dc in next dc,
*ch 1, dc in 2nd dc of next Shell,
ch 1, dc in 4th dc of same Shell,
ch 1, dc in 1st dc of next V-st,
ch 1, dc in 2nd dc of V-st;
rep from * across to last 2 dc,
ch 1, skip next dc, dc in last dc.
Break CC 2 and fasten off.

Border:
With right side facing, join MC with a
sl st in corner sp of upper right corner.
Rnd 1: Ch 1, 6 sc in same sp, now
working across last row, 2 sc in
each ch-1 sp, 6 sc in next corner sp,
working into ends of rows along side
edge, work 2 sc around each dc,
work 6 sc in corner sp,
working across beg ch,
work 2 sc in each skipped ch between
dc, work 6 sc in corner sp, work across
opposite side edge as before, join
with sl st to 1st sc.
Rnd 2: Ch 4, dc in same st,
*skip next 2 sc, V-st in next sc;
rep from * around, adjusting
skipped sts if necessary at
end of rnd, join with sl st in 3rd ch
of beg ch-4.

Designed by
Janetta Graber

Rnd 3: Sl st into next V-st, (ch 4, dc) in same sp, *V-st in next V-st; rep from * around, join with sl st in 3rd ch of beg ch-4.

Rnd 4: As Rnd 3.

Rnd 5: Sl st into next V-st, ch 5, *sc in next V-st, ch 5; rep from * around, ending last rep with ch 2, dc in base of beg ch-5 to form last ch-5 loop.

Rnds 6-8: Ch 1, sc in same loop, *ch 5, sc in next ch-5 loop; rep from * around, ending last rep with ch 2, dc in first sc, changing to CC 2 in last loop of dc.

Rnd 9: Using CC 2, ch 1, sc in same loop, *ch 6, sc in next ch-5 loop; rep from * around, join with sl st in 1st sc.

Fasten off. Weave in all ends.

Hexagon Blanket

Shown on page 27.

SHOPPING LIST

Yarn (Dk/ Sport Weight)

[1.75 ounces, 171 yards
(50 grams, 158 meters) per ball]:

- ☐ White (MC) 5 balls
- ☐ Pink (CC 1) 2 balls
- ☐ Lilac (CC 2) 2 balls
- ☐ Yellow (CC 3) 2 balls
- ☐ Green (CC 4) 2 balls

Crochet Hook

- ☐ Size G-6 (4.0 mm)
  or size needed for gauge

SIZE INFORMATION

Size: 43" [109 cm] diameter

GAUGE INFORMATION

One repeat (shell plus sc) = 1.25"
[3 cm] and 5 rows to 2" [5 cm] and
each finished motif measures 4.75"
[12 cm] from edge to edge, both
using **suggested** hook or any size
hook which will give the correct stitch
gauge or tension.

── STITCH GUIDE ──

Beg dec Ch 3, [yo, insert hook and
draw up a loop, yo and draw through
2 loops on hook] twice all in same sp,
yo and draw through all 3 loops on
hook.

dc3tog [Yo, insert hook and draw
up a loop, yo and draw through 2
loops on hook] 3 times all in same
space, yo and draw through all 4 loops
on hook.

INSTRUCTIONS

To Make Motif: Ch 6, join with sl st to
form a ring.

Rnd 1: Work Beg dec in ring,
[ch 3, dc3tog in ring] 5 times, ch 1,
hdc in top of Beg dec (this forms
last ch-sp).

Rnd 2: Work Beg dec in joining sp,
*ch 3, (dc3tog, ch 3, dc3tog) in
next sp; rep from * 4 times more,
ch 3, dc3tog in joining sp, ch 1,
hdc in top of Beg dec.

Rnd 3: Work Beg dec in joining sp,
ch 3, dc3tog in next ch-sp,
*ch 3, [dc3tog, ch 3, dc3tog] in
next ch-sp, ch 3, dc3tog in
next ch-sp; rep from *
4 times more, ch 3, dc3tog in
first joining sp, ch 1,
hdc in top of Beg dec.

Rnd 4: Ch 3 (counts as dc), dc in
same sp, [3 dc in next ch-sp] twice,
*(2 dc, ch 3, 2 dc) in next ch-sp,
[3 dc in next ch-sp] twice;
rep from * 4 times more,
(2 dc, ch 3) in joining sp, join with sl st
in top of beg ch 3. Fasten off.

Make 24 Motifs using MC.
Make 3 Motifs in each of CC 1, 2 and 3.
Make 4 Motifs in CC 4.

To Assemble:
Use one CC 4 Motif as the center of
the blanket.
Sew 6 MC Motifs around outside
edges of the center motif.
Sew flat edges of Motifs together;
do not worry about fitting the
corners together exactly.
Alternating contrast colors
(our model, working clockwise, used
[Pink, Lilac, Green, and Yellow] 3 times),
sew 12 Motifs around the
outside edge of the MC round.
Sew 18 MC Motifs around the
outside edge of the last round.
Weave in all ends.
The blanket is now shaped as a large
hexagon, with *corner* Motifs having
two ch-3 sps between the seams, and
on each side there are 2 Motifs with
only one ch-3 corner between seams.

Border: With right side facing, join MC in a *corner Motif* at the 1st dc to the left of a seam.

Rnd 1: Ch 3 (counts as 1st dc), *dc in each dc to corner sp, (dc, ch 2, dc) in corner ch-3 sp - **Point made**, [dc in each dc to next corner sp, make Point, dc in each of next 10 dc, *yo, insert hook in last ch-3 sp of this motif and draw up a loop, yo and draw through 2 loops on hook, yo and insert hook in first ch-3 sp of next motif and draw up a loop, yo and draw through 2 loops on hook, yo and draw through all 3 loops on hook -* **Dec made]** 3 times; rep from * around, join with sl st in beg dc.

Rnd 2: Sl st to next dc, ch 3, *dc in each dc to Point, make Point in ch-2 sp, [dc in each dc to next Point, make Point in Point, dc in each of next 10 dc, *yo, insert hook in next dc and draw up a loop, yo and draw through 2 loops on hook, skip Dec from Rnd 1, yo, insert hook in next dc and draw up a loop, yo and draw through 2 loops, yo and draw through all 3 loops on hook -* **Dec made]** 3 times; rep from * around, ending last Dec in first skipped dc of 1st hexagon, join with sl st in beg dc. Break yarn and fasten off MC.

Rnd 3: Join CC 3 in next dc after joining for Rnd 2, ch 3, *dc in each dc to Point, make Point in Point, [dc in each dc to next Point, make Point in Point, dc in each of next 10 dc, work Dec as previous rnd] 3 times; rep from * around, ending last Dec in first skipped dc of 1st hexagon, join.

Rnd 4: Repeat Rnd 3. Break yarn and fasten off.

Rnds 5 and 6: Using CC 1, rep Rnd 3. At end of Rnd 6, break yarn and fasten off.

Rnds 7 and 8: Using CC 2, rep Rnd 3. At the end of Rnd 8, break yarn and fasten off.

Rnds 9 and 10: Using CC 4, rep Rnd 3. At the end of Rnd 10, break yarn and fasten off. Weave in all ends.

Checkered Baby Blanket

◼◼◼◻ INTERMEDIATE

SHOPPING LIST

Yarn (Worsted Weight)

[6 ounces, 315 yards
(170 grams, 388 meters) per skein]:

- ☐ White   3 skeins
- ☐ Pink   2 skeins

Crochet Hook

- ☐ Size H-8 (5.00 mm)
  or size needed for gauge

SIZE INFORMATION

Finished: 31" x 37" [79 x 94 cm]

GAUGE INFORMATION

16 sc and 16 rows to 4" [10 cm]
measured over pattern using
suggested hook or any size hook
which will give the correct stitch
gauge or tension.

─ STITCH GUIDE ─

Note: Blanket is made carrying both
colors as you work. Lay color not
being used across top of work, and
enclose by working each sc over
strand.

To change color: In last sc of previous
color, yo and draw up a loop, draw
new color through both loops on
hook to complete sc.
When starting a new color in next
row, change color in last sc of row.

INSTRUCTIONS

With White, ch 116, draw Pink through
last ch.

Row 1: Using White, ch 1, sc in 2nd ch
from hook and in each of next 4 ch,
*using Pink, sc in each of next 5 ch,
using White, sc in each of next 5 ch;
rep from * to end, turn. (115 sc)

Rows 2-5: Ch 1, *work 5 sc in White,
work 5 sc in Pink; rep from * to last
5 sts, work 5 sc in White, turn.

Rows 6-10: Ch 1, *work 5 sc in Pink,
work 5 sc in White; rep from * to last
5 sts, work 5 sc in Pink, turn.

Row 11: Work as Row 2.

Now rep Rows 2-11 for pattern,
12 times more, then Rows 2-5 once.
Do Not turn at end of last row worked.
Fasten off Pink, but keep White
attached for border.

Border:

Rnd 1: Ch 1, work 3 sc in corner,
now sc evenly around entire outside
edge of blanket, working same
number of sc on each side, working
3 sc in each corner, join with sl st to
first sc.

Rnds 2-5: Ch 1, sc in each sc around,
working 3 sc in center sc of each
corner, join with sl st to first sc.

Rnd 6: Ch 3, *skip next sc, sc in next sc,
ch 1; rep from * around, join with sl st
in 2nd ch of beg ch-3.

Rnd 7: Sc in next sc, *ch 1, sl st in
next ch-1 sp, sc in next sc; rep from *
around, ch 1, join with sl st in joining
sl st. Fasten off. Weave in all ends.

Designed by
Dorothy Warrell

General Instructions

ABBREVIATIONS

"	inches
beg	begin or beginning
CC	Contrast Color
ch	chain
cm	centimeters
dc	double crochet
dec	decrease or decreasing
gm	gram
hdc	half double crochet
inc	increase or increasing
MC	Main Color
mm	millimeter
rem	remain or remaining
rep	repeat
rnd(s)	round(s)
sc	single crochet
sl	slip
sp(s)	spaces(s)
st(s)	stitch(es)
tog	together
tr	treble crochet
yo	yarn over hook

* or ** work instructions following or between * or ** as many more times as indicated in addition to the first time.

() or [ ] work enclosed instructions as many times as specified by the number immediately following **or** work all enclosed instructions in the stitch or space indicated **or** contains explanatory remarks

( ) the number(s) given at the end of a row or round denote(s) the number of stitches or spaces you should have on that row or round.

■□□□ **BEGINNER**	Projects for first-time crocheters using basic stitches. Minimal shaping.
■■□□ **EASY**	Projects using yarn with basic stitches, repetitive stitch patterns, simple color changes, and simple shaping and finishing.
■■■□ **INTERMEDIATE**	Projects using a variety of techniques, such as basic lace patterns or color patterns, mid-level shaping and finishing.
■■■■ **EXPERIENCED**	Projects with intricate stitch patterns, techniques and dimension, such as non-repeating patterns, multi-color techniques, fine threads, small hooks, detailed shaping and refined finishing.

Yarn Weight Symbol & Names	LACE 0	SUPER FINE 1	FINE 2	LIGHT 3	MEDIUM 4	BULKY 5	SUPER BULKY 6	JUMBO 7
Type of Yarns in Category	Fingering, size 10 crochet thread	Sock, Fingering, Baby	Sport, Baby	DK, Light Worsted	Worsted, Afghan, Aran	Chunky, Craft, Rug	Super Bulky, Roving	Jumbo, Roving
Crochet Gauge* Ranges in Single Crochet to 4" (10 cm)	32-42 sts**	21-32 sts	16-20 sts	12-17 sts	11-14 sts	8-11 sts	6-9 sts	5 sts and fewer
Advised Hook Size Range	Steel*** 6 to 8, Regular hook B-1	B-1 to E-4	E-4 to 7	7 to I-9	I-9 to K-10½	K-10½ to M/N-13	M/N-13 to Q	Q and larger

*GUIDELINES ONLY: The chart above reflects the most commonly used gauges and hook sizes for specific yarn categories.

CROCHET TERMINOLOGY		
UNITED STATES		**INTERNATIONAL**
slip stitch (slip st)	=	single crochet (sc)
single crochet (sc)	=	double crochet (dc)
half double crochet (hdc)	=	half treble crochet (htr)
double crochet (dc)	=	treble crochet (tr)
treble crochet (tr)	=	double treble crochet (dtr)
double treble crochet (dtr)	=	triple treble crochet (ttr)
triple treble crochet (ttr)	=	quadruple treble crochet (qtr)
skip	=	miss

CROCHET HOOKS												
U.S.	B-1	C-2	D-3	E-4	F-5	G-6	7	H-8	I-9	J-10	K-10½	L-11	M/N-13
Metric - mm	2.25	2.75	3.25	3.5	3.75	4	4.5	5	5.5	6	6.5	8	9

Slip Knot

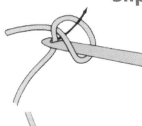

1. Make a loop, then hook another loop through it.

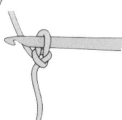

2. Tighten gently and slide the knot up to the hook.

Chain Stitch (ch)

1. Yarn over hook (yo) and draw the yarn through to form a new loop without tightening up the previous one.

2. Repeat to form as many chains (ch) as required. Do not count the slip knot as a stitch.

Slip Stitch (sl st)

This is the shortest crochet stitch and unlike other stitches is not used on its own to produce a fabric. It is used for joining, shaping and where necessary carrying the yarn to another part of the fabric for the next stage.

Insert hook into work (second chain from hook), yarn over hook (yo) and draw the yarn through both the work and loop on hook in one movement.

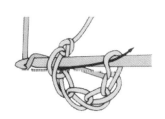

To join a chain ring with a slip stitch (sl st), insert hook into first chain (ch), yarn over hook (yo) and draw through both the work and the yarn on hook in one movement.

Single Crochet (sc)

1. Insert the hook into the work (2nd chain (ch) from hook on starting chain), *yarn over hook (yo) and draw yarn through the work only.

2. Yarn over hook (yo) again and draw the yarn through both loops on the hook.

3. 1 single crochet (sc) made. Insert hook into next stitch: repeat (rep) from * in step 1.

Half Double Crochet (hdc)

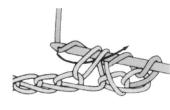

1. Yarn over hook (yo) and insert the hook into the work (3rd chain (ch) from hook on starting chain) and draw through the work only.

2. Yarn over hook (yo) again and draw through all three loops on the hook.

3. 1 hdc made. Yarn over hook (yo), insert hook into next stitch (st), draw through the work only, repeat (rep) from step 2.

Double Crochet (dc)

1. Yarn over hook (yo) and insert the hook into the work (4th chain from hook on starting chain) and draw through the work only.

2. Yarn over hook (yo) and draw through the first two loops only.

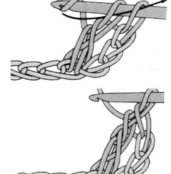

3. Yarn over hook (yo) and draw through the last two loops on the hook.

4. 1 dc made. Yarn over hook (yo), insert hook into next stitch (st) and draw through the work only; repeat (rep) from step 2.

Treble Crochet (tr)

Work same as given for Double Crochet (dc) above,
but in Step 1 yarn over hook (yo) twice, then rep Step 2 twice.

Yarn Information

Projects in this book were made with different weight yarns. Any brand of yarn may be used.
It is best to refer to yardage/meters when determining how many balls or skeins to purchase.
Remember, to arrive at the finished size, it is the GAUGE that is important, not the brand of yarn.
For your convenience, listed below are the specific yarn ranges used to create our photographed models.

Baby Flowers Blanket
Mary Maxim's Ultra Mellowspun

Dreamy Baby Blanket
Mary Maxim's Baby's Best

Cushy Crocheted Blanket
Mary Maxim's Baby Value

Candy Stripes Blanket
Mary Maxim's Baby Lollipop

Bavarian Baby Blanket
Mary Maxim's Ultra Mellowspun

Little Boy Blue Blanket
Red Heart Super Saver

Baby Pineapples Blanket
Mary Maxim's Baby's Best

Hexagon Blanket
Mary Maxim's Baby's Best

Checkered Baby Blanket
Caron's Simply Soft